# The Infinite Wealth Strategy: Unveiling the Secrets of The Rich

# Table of Contents

liveiws.com

liveiws.com

Everyone wants to become rich; everyone tries to become rich but have you ever wondered why most can never seem to get ahead? Why does your hard work get underrated, and you don't even receive the deserving income? Do you get paid what you are worth? I doubt it!

For that income, you work so hard in your life that you forget about your health and sometimes sacrifice the love for your family and friends. You know why? Because the financial system is rigged, and it seems very trappy. If you trace down the history of financial corruption, you will know how an ordinary person just like you and me is being exploited in the hands of a few who own the whole financial system.

It sounds so manipulative, but the truth has been kept hidden all our lives by a handful of super wealthy families who created this system of corruption. Even our previous generations had no clue about this unethical practice, or maybe they never thought of it ever happening to them. But it's time we should talk about it and bring it out into the light. Let's uncover those unaddressed questions regarding the worst financial lobby in history and change the banking system by replacing it with a new one.

## What is the Rigged System of finance all about?

This book is to make you aware and pull you out of the standard financial system. That is the "rigged system." It is a system where the bank has all the power, and you have none. They can charge high-interest rates, give out loans with hefty fees, and make it difficult for people to get their money back from them.

It can lead to people being in debt for years or even decades at a time. This debt has buried a million families under it, resulting in undeserving suffering.

It revolves around two things. The first one is TAX, and the second is INTEREST. We all are familiar with these two terms. These two words are a curse, but they are shown to us as if they are meant for our benefit. I know some of you may wonder why I call these terms 'harmful' while the government offered us the same in a 'good light.'

They are the foundational values that run the rigged system of finance. In my opinion, both should be banned, and we as ordinary people should go into depth to study why these two words and their existence is dangerous for a progressive society. Though the fact is that we live with them, and if we don't adhere to them, we are punishable. The banks live by a separate set of rules. They can create money out of nothing and if we do that we would go to prison! Fair? Ummm.. I think NOT!

## Bank Vs. Us

This rigged system is designed for the banks to win and for you to lose. Is it like a battle that we are fighting, where we are helpless and rich are dominating us with all their superpowers!

Now, why are interest and taxes not suitable for us, and why am I constantly urging clients to 'avoid' them? Understand it this way. The banks charge interest which is called USURY which used to be illegal. Usury historically has been banned and outlawed in most countries and wasn't practiced in human society except in the last few thousand years.

Taxes used to never exist and were implemented to fund war in recent times.

Even when the war was over, the illegal tax remained! It gets even worse. So, ultimately, it's you who is on the edge of the sword, and the other side has nothing to lose. The wool has been pulled over your eyes by the wealthy power-hungry crooks, and all we could do, obey them!

## The rich eat ice cream while the common starves until death.

In the U.S. financial system, there is a hierarchy. A hierarchy decides who takes what proportion out of the common man's hard work. It is a chronic problem that runs in the nation. The wealthiest strata include the mega-rich, politicians, and bank owners. These three layers make the rules and regulate the financial system.

Some of you may be aware that the politicians don't make the rules; they are influenced to make the rules. They are simply paid puppets. Technically, we expect politicians to develop practices that benefit society as a whole, but it is not true since the ones who control the money make the rules. The politician just blends them in financial language to trick all of us to do the will of the higher powers.

*He who controls the money supply controls the power.*

## How are we conditioned to give up our financial rights since birth?

Let's understand this with a simple example. Try to imagine it while reading further. When you are born, you are thrust into the rigged system by force of law. How? The government issues you a 'Birth Certificate' and a social security number (google why your name is in all CAPS, it may reveal some surprising insights for you.) The government looks at you as a corporation, not a person. It starts here, and it goes until you die. You are just a number and a business to the ones who control the system.

Every human being now just becomes simply a value. You are expected to go to school, learn how to read and write, develop a skill so you can earn a paycheck so you can pay taxes and also don't forget in most cases you are also forced to contribute to the governments 'qualified' retirement programs. Who controls that? Exactly I hope you get the point. Your role in life from their perspective is to work so they can create more power. It's all rigged!

## What were you not told by the Rich and the Government!

We all have learned financial fundamentals and have read financial bibles, but did anyone teach you financial literacy? What is financial literacy? Financial literacy is the knowledge and skills people need to make sound decisions about money management. It includes understanding concepts such as interest rates, inflation, credit cards, mortgages, savings accounts, stocks, and bonds. These are all examples of financial ideas that come into play when deciding how to manage your money. Financial literacy helps you understand the importance of savings, knowing how to budget and manage your money. Do you know you can make good decisions about the financial products you're offered and apply a basic understanding of investments, savings plans, loans, and mortgages to upscale your financial strategies? But no one has told this to you yet! Has anyone told you that you have a choice to OPT-OUT of the rigged system? Keep reading!

We weren't taught financial literacy; instead, we were piled up with economic laws. Financial literacy was removed from textbooks as this information is still NOT taught in school. The rigged system is doing its job by creating ignorant people who don't understand the rules of the game they were forced to play.

This is why I am writing this book! This information will change society and end poverty. This information gives every family a winning chance in life to succeed. Imagine a world with no poverty. This is not a world that the Elite want. They want slaves not free people.

Tell me, how early did you start acknowledging financial literacy and viewed it as a medium to help and not something to be scared of. Obviously if you're reading this book you're open enough to see why things are the way they are.

Governments have always created fear amongst the people that finance is dangerous to play with. Only those who have specialization can understand and evaluate it. But, it's not the truth. It's the half-told manipulation by those who control our money. We can all learn financial management, and it doesn't even require a degree. All the big shots in the world did not go to a finance school; they all learned to master money management by doing it.

## So, how can you change the rotten financial system?

Through Infinite Wealth Strategist's Vortex Banking System! That is why I am writing this book to share what I learned along my journey! I have made millions and lost millions, and now with the discovery of 2 powerful financial tools that the wealthiest families in the world still use to this day and have used for 100's and 100's of years, I am going to share with you some relevant information that exposes the rules to the game. If you know the rules you can learn to win the game.

*Open your mind to these concepts! Your mind is like a parachute. It only works when it's open.*

Can you answer me a simple question? Would you ever like to work for free? What if someone tells you to give 8 hours every day to a job that pays you nothing? Would you ever want to take a job like this? I believe no one will go through such exploitation.

Why? Because your time is valuable, right? You don't work for free! You have to pay your bills and provide for yourself and possibly, in most cases, take care of a family, right! But why am I asking you this obvious question? It is because sometimes we can't look beyond the curtain. If you can't take this exploitation, how come you are OK with the same old financial system exploiting us for years? Why do we continue to participate in a system that seeks to exploit us?

**Let me bombard you with another example:**

We have all seen a dollar. We love dollars, and all the hard work we do is because of that dollar. What is a dollar anyway? We have been taught one thing but what it actually is are two different things. There are two completely contrasting perspectives involved. We now see that the money system we have all been taught has been one big deception. We are all just spokes in someone else's wheel.

We have been taught that we have to exchange time for money in order to buy goods and services, money being the means of exchange, money that is used for trade. Everything is centered around money. Even in a room full of mega-rich people, the one with more money will always have more control. Right?

True, but you're only taught half the story. See, the ones who print the money created the lie and perpetuated that lie by creating the FED (The Federal Reserve System). They hold all the power! Not the ones with the money, you see? America's doomsday. The day we became a slave to a fiat currency-based system of capital slavery. Beholden to the banks and corruption of Wall Street and political Greed. In simple words this is when we lost our rights to people who 'seemed' more powerful.

We were fooled, and nobody knew the other side. Your perception of money is your reality of it as well. If you believe money is only to buy stuff, that all your money will do! Again, it all starts with your perception of money. Your thoughts become your reality. Change your thoughts about money and your results will change. By the end of this book I hope to have reprogrammed the way you see and think about money! It's time to wipe the hard drive and start new.

The ones who control the information being given on the subject of money control the perception of the people being taught. The ones that have more money, have more information, more knowledge, and more experience. All these together dominated the ones who thought they knew nothing about finance.

Control perception, control the world's reality. Control the world's reality, control the world.

# Fiat, FED, and everything else that controls our money and decisions!

Keep your eyes open because this will shake the entire foundation of your belief in the system. The truth no one else seems to want you to know, let alone how to accomplish it. Money is a debt instrument created to enslave you and your family. How? It was created for one purpose: to control and dominate. Now let's discuss how it all works. Let's discuss what money actually is.

Money, not in the form of physical currency like gold but the 'Monopoly Money,' is the money that we currently are using to buy, sell, trade, and invest. It's a means of control. Control through usury. See the FED prints money and loans it to the bank with debt interest. The banks then create loans with interest and push the debt into the economy to businesses through corporate finance. This cycle continues, but who is getting affected or who is at the target of their monopoly money? It's us. We are the ones who they are exploiting. Think how?

We leave our families and lives to trade our time for money, to build those corporations and make them money to pay back their loans with interest to the FED, and we earn a paycheck as the employee. See where this is going? We are earning for those who are printing money already!

This sounds like a crazy trap. It's so surprising to see how in bulk, we all are creating more money to give it back to those who are creating it already. This is a vicious cycle that is nothing less than playing a mind game.

We have all been a part of this since December 3rd 1913 when the FED was created. All generations did it: our parents, grandparents, and their parents. So, this is how it goes! We open a bank account and deposit our check. We then get a savings account and save. We get a debit card, checkbook to pay bills, and even a credit card! Now we are trapped! Their plan seems so perfect.

Now you have to pay your electricity bill which is 8 hours of work, insurance and car payment which is three day's worth of work. Mortgage, 2 weeks' worth of work. Groceries, 2 days' worth of work. Are you getting my point? We are working significant hours just for monopoly money.

I am trying to explain that after 80-120 hours of work every 2 weeks, we receive our income. We then deposit that income in the bank account, which by the way, has your time attached to it, the time you will never return to your kids, or family, ministry, or loved ones.

*Money equals your time!*

Now that money has left your account, you have to go sacrifice more time to earn it all over again. The cycle repeats and the bankers and elite win. We lose.

*Robert Kiyosaki calls it the rat race. I call it the 'rigged system.'*

You're shoved into it the day you're born when you're given a social security number and a name. You now have your GPS tracker, so every-time you handle money, banks can take what they call their 'fair share.' Fair share? Last I checked, if it's my time sacrificed to earn money, my fair share is 100%, and the government is 0! What did the government do to deserve part of my hard work? Now I'm all for some taxes to help society and make life better for the whole but NOT these obsessive taxes made to keep us under their feet!

# How the system scams you?

Here's what happens! The bank pays very little interest to the FED. They loan the money to corporations at interest (more than they have to pay back to the FED, so they profit.) So, they create more money out of thin air and then charge interest on this air. This is illegal, yet the FED does it every day. Now, you deposit your paycheck. The FED allows the bank through Fractional Reserve Banking to hold 10% of your deposit, and through a ledger system, they can create new money with the other 90%! Does it sound confusing? That is by design.

Understand it this way. You have given $100 to the bank. The bank then keeps only $10 in the vault, and the rest, $90, is loaned out, and the bank charges interest on it. It's your money but the bank plays with it.

A few questions to ask:

- Did you ever get any of that interest?
- Did you ask your bank where that interest has gone?
- Did your bank ever send you a check in the mail for dividends?
- Did your bank inform you of anything regarding this?

*No, right! Mine hasn't! So, the bank wins again!*

Now you run low on cash, so you have to tap your credit card. Now, you have to trade more time to pay that back, plus more interest! Think about it. The bank gave you a plastic card with fake monopoly money created by your efforts and sacrifices, and now you have to work harder and longer to pay it back. The whole process repeats in a vicious cycle of insanity. Insanity is doing the same thing over and over again expecting a different result. Do you like

liveiws.com

being insane? Me either so STOP! How might you ask? Knowledge! Keep Reading....

So Why then? Why do we struggle on our end when we do all the hard work? We deserve the pay, but all we get is nothing but more hard work and more pain? When you work for money, you make $100, and the bank makes $190!! How is this fair? How is this legal? Do the politicians who created this system play by its rules? No, never! They play by different rules made by them, for them.

## Is it over? Not yet!

We are almost getting to the solution but let's continue to face the facts! It gets worse. The banks take about 25% of their tier one capital, they would do more but the government restricts them, I'll go more into that later, and they buy 'BOLI,' Bank Owned Life Insurance. This allows them to earn tax-free gains on their money and get additional access to capital through the insurance carriers. Who do you think bails out banks and businesses during economic collapses? Yup! Insurance carriers! So again, the crooks make money.

The banks also do bad loans, bad mortgages and write off billions in bad debt; they knowingly created all while lives are ruined, people are homeless, and in some cases turn to crime, drugs, and in bad cases, suicide. As long as Wall Street makes its money, though, who cares, right? Hell no!

Imagine how we work; they gain, we lose, they make!

# The way out or the 'Secret of Escaping the Elite Trap.'

Now let's understand that we have a way out. We have hope to beat this trap and shed light to our upcoming generations and ourselves.

See, the Elites wrote the tax code, and within it, they wrote rules they all use legally to avoid paying interest and taxes allowing them to earn it all while 'avoiding' not 'evading' because that would be illegal, and they can't break the law. So, they wrote into the tax code one set of rules for us and one set for them. Why divide? When we are in society and live together, thrive together, then why does such a difference exist? Again it all comes down to power and control over humanity through USARY.

Here's the root of it all. Here's a perfect plan to self-perpetuate the lie. The government creates 'licenses' and programs to 'train' financial advisors, tax preparers, CPA's and all their other henchmen. They pay the government to get a license to 'advise' people on investing and taxes and so forth. The government creates the 'content' (brainwashing program) and teaches the 'professionals.' These people now come and perpetuate the 'Rigged System.' We follow orders and do what the pros tell us! After all they have a license, right? They are fresh out of class but ready to handle our money? We are told to give to a 401k, pay our taxes like good little sheep and don't question anything.

This just carries on, no questions asked. We teach our kids, and they teach their kids, and the lie continues for generations, and the elite maintains power over our lives. You now work for 40-50 years! Really?

That is NOT what life is for! Then how do we retire? Do you know anyone who's retired on 401k? No why? Taxes. These programs are deferred so when you take your money you are taxed! How do you know taxes won't be higher later in life?I'd rather be taxed on the seed NOT the harvest. So there is a better way and it's called Vortex Banking.

## What is Vortex Banking, and how is it creating wealth for a common man?

What if I told you there's a better way? What if you could exit this rigged system and create your own family economy that wasn't impacted by outside forces like the stock market? What if your money was safe in a titanium vault where it grew tax-free 24-7 where YOU could have control and power over your wealth where it really belongs.

Who's better with your money? You or the government? I think I know your answer.

In your family's hands, not the government and dirty politicians who created the problem.

Would you want to know how to escape this financial hell? Believe me; I am here to tell you how we can completely eliminate the monopoly money power owned by the rich.

Maybe some ears won't like to hear this, but I am 101% sure that this will change everything for you from now forward!

## Why should you believe me?

Elite families buried this knowledge for centuries but I found it! I implemented it. It works, and now

I'm teaching it to as many families and businesses as I can. It's time we stand up and play by the rules the rule-makers made. It's time our families take back the control that is rightfully ours and that was stolen through illegal policies passed at the highest levels of a failed economic system. The people can take a stand and use their own weapons against them and finally prosper.

I want to introduce you to Vortex Banking. Vortex Banking is a highly sophisticated financial strategy that only the MEGA Wealthy have utilized for almost 500 years! You can't even imagine the amount of money they have stolen from us. See, it's simply that the money game has rules. If you learn the rules you have a chance to play to win. Sadly though, most people are already too conditioned by the brain washing system to break free and actually think for themselves!

Just like a sport you're unfamiliar with, you wouldn't stand a chance playing with skilled players if you have never played the game.

If you're laughing in agreement, then take a look at how most of us play the money game without even knowing it! We play against sophisticated players, the bankers, who make the rules, yet we wonder why we are always on the losing end, it seems! Try to relate this with a common example. When you are not a pro at something, you tend to lose at it. This is to be expected. Now if the rules to the game are hidden from you, you never stand a chance do you?

Even if you WIN big, for example, in Real Estate, Uncle Sam is there awaiting his TIP! It's called Capital Gains! That's how the government welcomes your success, TAXES! The Vortex will protect you from these slimy weasels. Keep reading. It's coming.

## *The dirty game of interest.*

Albert Einstein once said, "Compound Interest is the eighth wonder of the world. Those who understand it earn it, those who don't pay it!" You would think the eighth wonder of the world would be some magnificent structure we stand in awe of, BUT nope, one of the smartest men to walk this earth said YOU need to understand compound interest! This intrigued me to the point I believed him! I went on a journey to understand how interest works and man was I blown away. Where was this class in school?

So, the point is, two things we need to get a handle on are understanding are interest and taxes and how to legally AVOID paying what we don't have to. These 2 things are how the system fleeces our families and we have to get these in OUR CONTROL.

Don't you think it's possible? I know some reading this think it's all BS! If that's you, then the rigged system is working just as it was designed. You are a good little sheeple and the government would like to give you a fake gold star.

If you're curious like I was, keep reading. It's about to get EVEN MORE INTERESTING! I want to recap again how banks earn money because in order to play the game, we need to become the bank!

## How do banks make money?

Fractional Reserve Banking is one of the most popular ways how banks make money!

Fractional-reserve banking - the most common form of banking practiced by commercial banks. Only a fraction of bank deposits are backed by actual cash on hand, so this portion of the money is available for withdrawal.

Remember the $100 example I gave before where your $90 dollars was loaned out and charged interest? It gets even better when the bank uses your $100 that you earned to create more money out of thin air by multiplying your deposit, creating new money that doesn't even exist! How is this fair? If we created money out of thin air, we would go to prison, yet banks do it every day. Now without understanding the rules, you WILL lose every time!

It may seem like you win once in a while but remember the experts you're playing against made the rules, unless you know when you don't stand a chance.

Now that we have covered the importance of understanding compound growth and how banks make money, let's talk about how we can position our families to BE THE BANK to create a system where our deposits can earn interest for us rather than the greedy bankers. How amazing would it be to create a system for free that allows every dollar you earn to earn guaranteed interest for the rest of your life, all tax free? If that sounds interesting keep reading!

The bankers have always overpowered us with the sword in their hands, but today, you don't have to worry about their mere existence. Your bank will no longer be run by your bankers but by you!

## The answer is - Learn the rules!

SO, we need our income to earn compound interest. Where can we put our income where it will grow, preferably tax-free, while still having complete access to the funds so you can continue to live, work, eat and invest!

Families like the Rockefellers, the Disney's, and the Buffets have been using a highly sophisticated tool for hundreds of years, and it's been right under our nose the whole time! As a matter of fact, I think you'll agree by the end of the book that it's internationally been hidden from the general population.

We use a highly sophisticated, specially engineered Whole Life Policy with a Mutual Company that pays dividends. This also needs to be a NON-Direct Recognition company, and I will explain more shortly. I know if you're like me right now your saying Life Insurance? Believe me I know but when I'm done explaining this, trust me you won't sleep!

We call this a LiveIWS Banking Policy. When you deposit money into a banking policy, you earn a guaranteed % plus potential dividends when with a mutual or fraternal company. You're already doing better than the bank day one! These policies are not like traditional old school whole life policies. These are cash producing policies that allow you to access most of the premium you pay from day one without sacrificing your ability to earn interest! It's literally insuring your income!

We insure everything else. Cars, homes, pets... Why weren't we taught to use insurance to insure the most important thing we have! Our life and our income!

Now for the engine that makes this all work. Remember I said Non-Direct Recognition. This becomes very important right here.

Let's say I need to pay bills. If I take the income that I worked for and deposit it into my traditional bank, I deposited my income and all the hours it took to make that income. Now I go home and take my debit card and pay my cell phone bill.

When we use this system, we essentially just gave the phone company part of our income, and all the time it took us to make that income. So, what do we have left? A working cell phone for another month but NO money and NO time. Got to go back to work and start over again!

But here is a better way. The way the Elite don't want you to know. Once you have a LiveIWS banking Policy set up, You now take part of your income, deposit it into YOUR new bank. Here, the LiveIWSsytem has a death benefit that your traditional bank did not. The insurance carrier allows you to use your cash deposits as collateral to borrow against the insurance companies general fund! It means that your physical cash STAYS inside YOUR BANK, earning "Uninterrupted" compound growth. It is due to the non-direct status of the carrier. It means you can borrow against your cash value without being penalized! Isn't this what Albert Einstein was talking about? Now your money is earning interest, uninterrupted, in a tax free environment while still giving you access to live your life as usual! This is a game changer!

Let's evaluate this one with an example. If you have $50k in cash value and borrow out $25K, you are still earning interest on the entire 50k! Is this surprising for you? What happened here is that they didn't recognize the loan on the balance where I am earning interest. Why? They have my collateral already. You can always borrow up to your cash value, and this includes all your deposits PLUS the % you earn in interest and the potential dividends! It allows you to recapture and recycle your money over and over again in a closed-looped system! This is how the wealthiest families around the world have continued to build wealth generation after generation.

It is how the wealthy build wealth, and now, you can too. Your money is now working for you in a system 24/7, all while still being able to utilize your dollars. Imagine you borrow $50k from your bank to invest in Real Estate. Let's say you do a house flip and make a 12% profit. If you used your LiveIWS Banking System, add another 4-6% to that because NOW your money is working in 2 places at one time. That is called leverage. Wealth is created by leveraging your money and now you have leverage.

*This may sound new to you, but it really works.*

If you are not insuring your TIME and MONEY, you are not creating enough wealth for yourself!

We all understand insurance. I'll say it again to drive the point home. We insure our cars, homes, pets, and health, but why not our TIME & MONEY? Isn't this the most important thing to protect? You pay for all of this insurance, and what do you get for it? In most cases, NOTHING! We were never told that money and time run parallel, and as a human, one should not value them in meanings only but also in monetary terms.

Why not insure your income so if times get tough, which they always do, you have a system in place that protects you and your family from hard times! During the COVID crisis recently, look how many families and small businesses lost everything from the lockdowns and the inability to generate revenue! Imagine if they had this system set up and could tap into their LiveIWS Banking System to survive and even continue to thrive! We could have saved millions of families going under debt and money torture. Our clients were protected during this crisis.

I hope you have understood this: all till now. See, you have to learn about the rules folks. The game is simple, but if you aren't well versed with the rules, you may still struggle to make it big. Do you realize that if you take the information I'm sharing with you and apply it, you're creating a NEW LEGACY for your future family and many generations to come? Your entire family tree will drastically change because of the applied knowledge you gained from this book. I am giving you the keys to the kingdom, and all you have to do is the application!

So again we can eliminate interest by using the LIVEIWS Banking System to become our own bank. We can now use our own system to borrow from to make purchases and then pay ourselves back where we now earn the interest on our own money! Go buy a car with your bank, pay the payments each month back to yourself and you'll end up with the money and the car at the end of it! Imagine buying a car where the money you used to purchase it was still earning interest while you were driving the car! No longer will you need the traditional bank and no longer do we have to pay high interest charges to the crooks! We keep our money and we keep our interest in our own system creating even more wealth!

See your bank makes money! It's a business and you're now the client and the bank. The money the bank was making on you is now earned and captured in YOUR BANK! Now, let's move on to the big one. The bad word we all can't stand. Just hearing it makes us all feel a certain way. TAXES.

EVADING TAXES IS ILLEGAL BUT AVOIDING TAXES IS OUR RIGHT!

What I am about to share with you is almost taboo to discuss. Taxes are what makes the Elite who they are. It's their biggest weapon of control so very few people will even write about this topic. There is a tool that has existed since the 1400's and was created in Europe to protect land that was being seized by kings. It's a special type of trust that probably less than 2% of the population even knows exists. This tool has since come to America and now even includes the IRS code that is written into the trust document giving even more power to impact taxes.

I'm talking about a tool that is like a titanium vault when it comes to asset protection (preserving wealth), anonymity and well as the ability to defer tax in most cases in perpetuity. 100% legally while complying with IRS code as well as Scott on Trust Law.

Our Trust is a non-grantor, irrevocable, complex, discretionary, Spendthrift Trust which is copyrighted. Let's talk about what all this means.

## WHAT IS A Spendthrift TRUST?

Trusts legal entities that can be used to transfer and manage property or assets. It is an ingenious entity empowering Trustees of the Trust to have and hold all control over that property or assets. The terms and conditions of the Trust strictly define the form of the trust used and the needs of the people it is created to serve.

Trust Establishment Consideration of some type is transferred from a Settlor to another person (known as the trustee) with the understanding that the recipient will hold the property and assets or use them in a way that is directed or established as laid out in the terms and conditions of the trust. Anyone who benefits from the use of the property or assets is known as the beneficiary.

Trust Estate. The property or assets that are transferred to a trust becomes the trust corpus. The Trustee of a trust is the only entity that can affect the transfer of assets, property or monies to a trust. A trust estate consists of all of the property (tangible or intangible), assets, cash, rights and obligations that are transferred to the trust. The trust estate is managed in accordance with the terms and conditions of the documents creating the trust. Because the property is held in trust it is generally not subject to turnover*.

Parties to a Trust.

The SETTLOR sometimes called the Creator, Grantor, Settlor or Trustor, is any person who creates a trust for the benefit of beneficiaries. To establish the trust, and realize the protection afforded, the trust should be established through an initial funding by a settlor, someone who cannot be the trustee or the beneficiary. After the trust is established, the trustee may convey additional assets, tangible and intangible, to the trust for the benefit of the beneficiaries.

The TRUSTEE is a person, financial institution (such as a bank or trust company) or managing entity that holds the legal title in trust for the trust estate. There may be one or more trustees. If a trustee is unable or unwilling to serve then a successor trustee steps in to hold and manage the trust estate. The trustee is obligated to act in accordance with the terms and conditions of the trust for the benefit of the trust beneficiaries.

The BENEFICIARIES are the persons or entities which benefit from the trust estate. The rights of beneficiaries depend on the terms and conditions of the trust. Beneficiaries have no "equitable title" only a "beneficial interest" in the property or assets held in the trust. Beneficiaries have no right of management of the trust nor have any right to have access to business records or knowledge of trust business or actions.

*There are limited exceptions to being protected from creditors. It varies from state to state. For example, a statute in Texas allows a court to garnish child support payments from a spendthrift trust.

So now that you know the structure of the trust positions let's keep going.

*A practical approach: Vortex System and Infinite banking Strategy*

We have discussed taxes as a bad term above, but before you learn about Vortex Banking and Infinite Banking Strategy's magic, let's read why exactly I am against the Taxes.

It is a subject most want to 'Avoid " and avoid " it will, legally. It is a topic that the wealthy families have mastered to the point that the Rigged Economy doesn't really apply to them much.

# Well, how is that?

Nelson Rockefeller's famous quote, Own Nothing and Control Everything, is the key! If you don't own anything, how could you be taxed? Sued? How could anyone take something away from you that doesn't belong to you? Right. They Can't!

But then you might think that if you don't own anything, people will consider you poor. You don't have any wealth. But that's how the riches do! They don't own; they control. Pretty funny how the elite use word play. They use the word own for us and control for them? What is the difference? Big Difference!

Owning is the lie we bought. We are told to own things but with ownership comes the control and the liability!

## Ownership or control, which one will you choose?

What does it mean to control an asset? Pretty much the same thing as owning it except NO Liability! You get to enjoy the car, live in the home, fly in the private jet, swim in the pool without any liability of ownership. When the lawns need to be mowed, the Trust pays for it. When the roof needs to be replaced, the pool leaks, or the car tire is flat, you don't own the asset anymore, the Trust does, and it now pays for all of those expenses!

No one can sue you and take any asset that belongs to the Spendthrift trust. Now you have an iron-clad titanium vault protecting the assets and no taxes.

The purpose of telling you why taxes are not right for us is to make you understand the value of the Infinite Banking Strategy!

A trustee takes legal ownership of the assets held by a trust and assumes fiduciary responsibility for managing those assets and carrying out the Trust's purposes.

Understand it this way that the property or assets transferred to a trust will be accounted for in the trust corpus. The trustee remains the only entity with the right to transfer those assets, property, or monies to the beneficiary. The beneficiary is your children or grandchildren.

So what happens is that once you place those assets or money in the Trust, no one has the right to remove it from there. No court or any entity can remove them from the Trust. The spendthrift trust is indeed proven to withstand court judgments, lawsuits, bankruptcies, and divorces. These trusts have prevented creditors from attaching trust creditors. So, the Spendthrift Trust holds many potentials to safeguard your money and prevent you from going into debt. And most importantly, you are always controlling your wealth according to your terms and conditions even after you die. This is all because this trust operates under CONTRACT LAW not Legislative law. Big Difference.

There are a lot of things that one should know about Trusts. There are some facts and details that can help you understand why this Trust is for you and how it encourages a sustainable wealth process.

There are some important points that you have to take into account.

- The settlor has no rights at all. It doesn't even have a beneficial interest in the Trust.
- The trustee may disburse funds to the beneficiaries. It can be in equal amounts, unequal amounts, or not at all. It depends upon his/her absolute discretion.

- In the Trust Documents, beneficiaries can be anyone or any organization.

## What about the Taxes?

When some money or assets are provided to the Trust for it to be capitalized or endowed, there will be no taxable event. The Trust pays taxes on what those particular assets will earn. If needed, it can be paid to the trust corpus according to the terms and conditions. All the monies paid to beneficiaries are taxable. IWS Trust is a discretionary trust and in compliance with the IRS regulations.

The money that the Trust earns from the endowment funds remain undistributed to the beneficiary. But if there is any money that the trustee distributes to the beneficiary from the original endowment of the Trust, it becomes a non-taxable event for the Trust.

But a lot then depends on the terms and regulations of the Trust. For instance, the money that the Trust is earning can be taxable unless it is deemed to be paid to the trust corpus. These are some technical things that require careful handling of the taxes to get trapped in the vicious cycle of unwanted taxes.

However, the Spendthrift Trust is a complex trust, and it is not easy for anyone to prove it wrong since a solid strategy backs it. When the Trust is required to file federal income tax returns, form 1041 is used, but the Trust's capitalization and endowment are not at all taxable. They are retained indefinitely and can only be distributed by the trustees. These are not taxable events.

Here are some answers on the "Compliance Overseer."

- As long as he/she is not the settlor of the trust, he/she can be the trustee.
- One can always switch between the trustees.
- No matter if you hired someone before, but now you are willing to replace, you can do it easily.
- You can remove or appoint your beneficiary at any point in time or you.
- May never be a beneficiary.
- You can appoint your successor at any time during his lifetime.

It is important to note here that if the compliance overseer does not appoint any successor until the time of his/her death, then the office will disappear. The existing trustee and the beneficiary appointed remain the same.

# What other advantages does Spendthrift Trust have for you?

Do you know a Spendthrift trust is so lucrative to establish and can be easily maintained by you and involve minimal paperwork? You are not involved in complex jargon or anything. It also reduces fees, and in most cases, the fee gets eliminated completely. The trust is in compliance with the U.S. Constitution, Supreme Court, and other court decisions. It is lawful and guaranteed, so one has nothing to doubt for you. It is also lawful in every state of the U.S. The trust can easily operate from one state to the other. It breaks the restriction of movement.

How amazing is this to see that the trust actually works according to the rules and regulations of the U.S. laws? It has been made irrevocable to avoid any question regarding the ownership of the assets. One of the many great benefits of a trust is that it prevents the information from becoming public.

Anything shared by you is always kept private regarding assets, liabilities, and heirs. So, your trust in the trust is totally justifiable. Imagine that such advantages are totally helpful for you. Also, the trust can operate any lawful business anywhere in the world since it is liable and has benefits that every corporation has.

Since there is no paperwork involved and the Trust is not liable to answer any state or government, then periodic reporting and accounting culture also end with it. It is one of the best things that makes the Trust different from the standard financial system.

It provides you the same constitutional rights, just like an individual. The trust gives you all the basic rights that an individual has, like the right to privacy, freedom from search, and refrain from self-incrimination.

Remember that your personal BANKRUPTCY HAS NO EFFECT on the Spendthrift Trust assets. Absolutely no effect!

It can widely benefit everyone, be it people belonging from different professions like doctors, dentists, engineers, chiropractors, or anyone else: retired, investors, and foreigners. Almost everyone can benefit from this Trust.

So with a Spendthrift Trust, you can maintain privacy, eliminate your insurance liability, reduce income taxes and make a reverse financial investment. It has a wide scope to protect your income, and that's where you can save most of the money.

The Spendthrift Trust's main aim is to encourage one to live and manage their wealth the way they want to. There is absolute freedom in controlling your wealth. It is how the wealthy regulates their income and keeps their wealth alive for generations and generations. Also, people who are thinking reading this that if avoiding taxes is criminal, let me tell you it is NOT!

There are so many laws that defy this since the government only regulates the tax entities it creates, but, in this case, they aren't creating any tax entities. You should also understand that the Spendthrift Trust does not work according to the legislative laws, and thus it is more personalized. There is no magic wealth that you are creating; you are just multiplying the income in numbers with appropriate practices.

liveiws.com

To end this for now let's take a look at what the IRS says about IRSC643. This is the code written into the trust document.

# The Internal Revenue Code States Plainly

Internal Revenue TITLE 26, Subtitle A, CHAPTER 1, Subchapter J, PART I, Subpart A, Sec 643 (a)(3),(4),(7) and (b) states:

(3) Capital gains and losses. Gains from the sale or exchange of capital assets shall be excluded to the extent that such gains are allocated to corpus and are not (A) paid, credited, or required to be distributed to any beneficiary during the taxable year, or (B) paid, permanently set aside, or to be used for the purposes specified in section 642 (C). Losses from the sale or exchange of capital assets shall be

excluded, except to the extent such losses are taken into account in determining the amount of gains from the sale or exchange of capital assets which are paid, credited, or required to be distributed to any beneficiary during the taxable year. The exclusion under section 1202 shall not be taken into account.

(4) Extraordinary dividends and taxable stock dividends For purposes only of subpart B (relating to trusts which distribute current income only), there shall be excluded those items of gross income constituting extraordinary dividends or taxable stock dividends which the fiduciary, acting in good faith, does not pay or credit to any beneficiary by reason of his determination that such dividends are allocable to corpus under the terms of the governing instrument and applicable local law.

(7) Abusive transactions The Secretary shall prescribe such regulations as may be necessary or appropriate to carry out the purposes of this part,

including regulations to prevent avoidance of such purposes. If the estate or trust is allowed a deduction under section 642(c), the amount of the modifications specified in paragraphs (5) and (6) shall be reduced to the extent that the amount of income which is paid, permanently set aside, or to be used for the purposes specified in section 642(c) is deemed to consist of items specified in those paragraphs. For this purpose, such amount shall (in the absence of specific provisions in the governing instrument) be deemed to consist of the same proportion of each class of items of income of the estate or trust as the total of each class bears to the total of all classes. (b) Income for purposes of this subpart and subparts B, C, and D, the term "income", when not preceded by the words "taxable", "distributable net", "undistributed net", or "gross", means the amount of income of the estate or trust for the taxable year determined under the terms of the governing instrument and applicable local law. Items of gross income constituting extraordinary dividends or taxable stock dividends which the fiduciary, acting in good faith, determines to be allocable to corpus under the terms of the governing instrument and applicable local law shall not be considered income.

So now that we have covered the LiveIWS Banking system and how this is a proven way to eliminate paying interest ever again to a traditional bank, we have also covered the structure, capabilities and provisions of the Specialized Trust. Let's now pull it together and see how the Vortex really works.

*Having your own bank feels unrealistic, but it is actually HAPPENING!*

Vortex banking works like this. Our beneficial trust can defer all passive income NOT active income. Active income can be deferred through our business trust and we have some highly advanced strategies for that that I will save for a more in depth book. For now let's just look at the big picture.

The trust is in place and is now taking in income with the ability to defer. This includes Real Estate Investment income such as wholesaling, fix and flips, rental income and capital gains! Stocks and Crypto can also be owned by the trust as to avoid capital gains when sold.

Everything we own has been sold to the trust and now we have a demand note which is a legal IOU sitting in the trust for the sale of your assets. In other words the trust owes you still. Now we sell the LiveIWS Banking Policies on each family member to the trust.

The trust now owns that asset. Now that the trust owns the policy, remember that the trust can defer all passive income, life insurance is passive income. So what does this mean? It means your LiveIWS banking policy can now become even more efficient. For time sake I won't go deep here but with a whole life policy the government regulates how much profit you can gain until your taxes. This is called an MEC or modified endowment contract.

You do not want a MEC because you will get a 1099R from the carrier each year and be required to pay taxes on the capital gains. Now that you have a trust and the trust owns the policy, the trust will receive the 1099r and has the discretionary power to defer it! Do you get what I just said? If the trust owns it, it CAN BE a MEC and your bank will now get higher annual returns without the normal taxation on a MEC!

Also, when the trust owns the policy it is responsible to pay the premium with trust dollars which are deferred! Don't we usually pay life insurance with after tax dollars? Catching my drift?

See the Vortex allows passive income to go in, be deferred and then used to pay for trust expenses IE. Funding Your Bank! The trust can borrow against the policy and make investments where the money is now being leveraged in multiple places at the same time. This is how wealth is created and kept! It is a system.

Now what about personal funds. The only thing you need personal funds for now is food, fun and fashion. The trust cannot pay personal expenses. So we use the demand note for this. The IRS says taxes are paid when a distribution is made. The trustee has discretion to distribute or to not. Remember contract law not legislative.

If the trustee decides not to make a distribution but to draw down off their demand note, then no taxes would be due. The demand note becomes your personal account with the trust access dollars that do not need to be distributed. Everything you owned is now owned by the trust so those expenses are all paid by the trust. There is a lot more to this and much more you can do but again, this book is to share with you the concept and the rules and in a later book I'll break down the strategies and how to use them. I think you get the point now that when you have tools you have an advantage! It's time you load up your tool box and start learning how to live the way the wealthy families do and create your own financial economy that you control.

The effort at Infinite Wealth Strategist is to create a system for your family. It is a system that is not manhandled by any law, politician, or anyone sitting on the creamy layer. This system is not rigged. It is absolutely trustable, and moreover, it is created by you. If you have created this system, how come anyone else dominates it with monopoly power or selfish interest. As I said before, the Rigged system is not for us; it is for the benefit of the rich and the people who are running us.

All the financial laws created till now are not in our right, but they are made to give us just a portion of satisfaction. And look, we have been conditioned with it since the beginning. We think banks and all these financial crooks are working for us, but it's not. Though the common man is in the majority, what he receives is not even half of what he performs all his life. We now start considering it seriously and play the game by the rules. The rules are not the dirty secrets of riches but a straightforward way to build a fortune all by ourselves.

When you talk to an Infinite Banking Strategist, you are not talking to a company's employee; you are conversing with the person who is about to create your finance roadmap journey. It will help you open your own bank and cover the basic 5 things. From death, disability, retirement, long term care to tax efficiency, everything will be backed by the personalized bank.

Every person has individual needs and requirements, but the standard financial system does not work like this. It has no customized or personalized financial system. It remains the same for everyone. But with this financial roadmap, you have all the right to keep things your way.

The strategies we use are the same that the rich have been using for the last 500 years. Everything is created and designed according to what you plan. From little details to crucial wealth planning, the strategists always guide you with what's right and wrong for you.

You add more than one perspective to your wealth planning, but things work the way you want them to work; just like I told you before that when you own a bank, you run it according to you.

Our strategist designs your bank, and all you have to do is list down the important financial goals you have. The wealth strategist is your personalized bank engineer, and working with them can help you know many other things about creating wealth that has been hidden for a long from you.

With the help of a customized infinite banking strategy, you can control all your financial decisions and everything you wish to do in your financial life.

A proposal is made and then sent to you for reading and acknowledging. If you have any doubt or query, you can discuss this with your wealth strategist, and he/she can guide you for the same what I like the most about this system because you are not rushing into anything. There is passion, patience, and willingness to make the client understand everything in detail. Once you are done approving it and reviewing everything twice, we move on to the application process.

This application process has an application specialist. You see, no one person is guiding you throughout the system. The system enables you to break the bondage and get away with creditors and traditional banking practices.

Do you remember that we always wanted to do things our way in childhood, but our parents or mentors were always there to guide us? It is the same here. We are making our own financial decisions but with the help of those who are well-versed with personalized banking systems.

So basically, with the help of your own bank, you're creating wealth, funding it, and growing it all by yourself. The purpose of creating this bank is that I want you to manage your wealth so that you don't get misguided by people who have a selfish interest in your money.

# How do you create your own Financial Map? You Don't! We do it for you!

Well, everything is dependent on what level of the financial state you are at. What kind of wealth you have like assets, cash, property, etc. Once the financial mapping strategist evaluates your current wealth status, it becomes easy to set unique goals. These goals are like the guide map. Imagine them as the connecting dots. Every dot has a financial purpose and motive attached to it. Once all the information is collected and placed down on the map, you get a whole new financial roadmap ready for you.

It's not that you won't be having any pitfalls, problems, unexpected outcomes, or blocks, but that's not what you have to worry about. Every financial planning takes time and effort, and if you carefully plan to maneuver, it will succeed. How to save money or how to generate wealth will always be at the center of everything in our strategy. You will be able to see when exactly you will be debt-free.

This personalized financial strategy can be so helpful that it works beyond your imagination. It will tell you how much time it will take you to achieve your goals and how much money you can save along the way. Your assets and wealth will be protected by lawsuits, divorce, and judgments. You will also be able to avoid capital gains and escape estate taxes.

To my surprise, I was always told that if you are in debt, you can't save all your life. These two things can never run parallel. But I am happy to share with you that all that is absolutely wrong. People who are asking you to quit on your dreams because you are under debt, those people have already made millions by pulling down people like you. It is the time when you have to believe in whatever you have and create wealth out of it.

With this financial map, you have a clear picture of how your money will work for you and build your future. Also, the tax-free income and your dream retirement plans will become a possibility. So, waiting for your creditors to cheat you again is not something you have worked for. It is time that you protect your assets and grow your wealth.

It's so challenging sometimes because I have seen families losing their mental peace. Remember that it is your money, and no one can take that away from you unless you are willing or unknowingly most of the time just GIVE IT AWAY. With your new banking system, no taxes and no interest can vanish your worth.

Look, it's all about your financial goals and how you want to succeed. It's time that you take a step for yourself and your family to make all those dreams come true. But unless you won't be able to make up your mind, you won't be able to cover up for the loss. Most people fail from the start and the start is making a decision that will alter the course you are on.

Our wealth strategists can help you with the best financial strategies to be innovative in creating new wealth opportunities for you. All it takes is planning and execution, to begin with.

This system is highly advanced and created for your wealth convenience. So, ultimately, it's you, who controls the finance and not anyone else. Your money, you play by your rules in the game.

A while back, I used to think, what if we can create wealth on our own? And I was knocked down by many, but today, when I share this successful idea of genuine wealth creation, I feel overwhelmed to see so many people's life-changing experiences.

It's like a recipe that was hidden for a long time, and today it's out! All the ingredients are out. Now everyone can cook, share and taste it. This feeling is beyond an expression. I feel as if justice has been done now. This is no unique way of creating wealth. It has been running in the riches' blood for a lifetime now. So, it is a time tested and proven method that you can now have access to!

So, what's next? It's the LiveIWS Mapping that will make you understand how the system works in reality and what all is yet to discover.

There are so many threads attached to this one system. If you get to know why escaping the regular banking system is the goal, financial wisdom will come to you without much effort. Infinite Wealth

Strategist is not just a name; it has made a new reality for many families across the country.

I wonder how someone can be so selfish? Why did the creamy layer crooks never tell us this before? Why did we suffer so much at the hands of a few? Those who spoiled our lives through a scam rotten system should be locked in jail!

The LiveIWS Mapping is a key takeaway here. You need to have a plan and most people have none! They think a government retirement program will do the trick. Well they are in for a rude awakening and when that time finally arrives it will be too late. Now your older and after the crooks tax your retirement account you end up as a greeter at Walmart. Some may laugh at that but I seriously don't find that funny. It's sad.

liveiws.com

# Infinite Banking Strategy Mapping & The Broken System

I know that I have asked you to ask your banks. Ask your bank what they have done for you so far? Why was our hard work just peanuts all our lives? And honestly, I am scared about our upcoming generation, the generation that will work hard, sweat hard and receive nothing in return. The clarity through Infinite Banking Strategy Mapping gave me a way out, and here I am sharing the truth about the traditional banking system.

Every day you wake up, get ready, set your work calendar, start your car, take public transport, reach your office, and start working and working. You come back home stressed with incomplete deadlines and more work. You mug up your food, rush to your phone, start replying to emails and sleep tired. We all do this. The work culture has taken us for granted.

But have you ever calculated the value or return you are receiving on it? Maybe some of you must be earning amazing, and some of you are still barely making through essential expenses.

Now whatever you are earning, that amount is going to your bank accounts. It is your bank that is receiving your salary on your behalf. Even those savings you make are being deposited in the bank. So, in short, you can't even see the amount received in real life. If I throw some solid facts on you, like around 96% of Americans are going through financial illiteracy and you may be one of them, how would you react?

If I ask you some questions related to the basic financial literacy quiz, more than half of you will not attempt, and those who will, are more likely to fail or score really low. In reality, around 60% of Americans don't have enough cash to pay for a $400 emergency, and 53% of student loan borrowers cannot make payments. This is such a disgusting statistic to believe, but it is the truth. Not just this, but 65% of Americans are under credit card debt, and 87% have no or little savings while going through retirement. Numbers don't lie, people do.

Why do we still trust a system that leaves us with nothing in the end except disappointments? Even when we are supposed to rest and live in peace, we are forced for every single penny even after our last breath by the scavengers? Is that the return we get after working like crazy in our life? It isn't good to see a system that talks about the so-called American dreams but is not even close to it.

These figures don't lie, pointing to the brutality of the centuries-old system that was made to exploit common aspirations under the selfish means of the rich.

No, I am not being rude here. It is my disappointment with the system. A system that always demanded us to be educated, but it never taught us the value of financial literacy. It is the reason why we never felt that our finances reflect our efforts. We started believing that whatever is happening to us is right. But I don't want to get deep into this right now, maybe in some other book. Right now, the focus is to tell you how to come out of the system and make your own financial rules. You now have the power to take back the control that was stolen from you long ago.

Let's get rid of this broken financial system, a system where up to 75% of your annual income is absorbed by 3rd party creditors or the IRS. And you don't even know why are you paying them?

You do the hard work, and they get the money. That is a major chunk of your income. I can't stop talking about those various tricks played by the system runners on you. It's like since the beginning, things have turned out in their favor always. We were the ones unaware on the other side of the table. But again now you know it is by design. There is no more making excuses for staying stuck. You know the truth now.

It is in our financial culture, a culture where we have to warehouse our money within the traditional banking system made by the banking officials and governments to fool us. We are scared to death in doing anything that goes against the system. At the same time, the truth is that the rich who are debted with incredible loan amounts are freed by the banks for their selfish interests.

And we rely on risky investment policies for retirement plans and can't even afford a life without debt. It is such a bad broken financial cycle that is destroying us both financially and mentally. It drains all our energy since money plays an important part in penetrating peace in our lives.

Without money, we end up with the worst of thoughts. Just like we need air to survive, we also need money to survive. It's the lifestyle demanded today. You go anywhere in the world; money will always be the center of everything. Money is more than a currency today. It is a necessity. Zig Ziglar said "Money is like oxygen, everyone needs it!"

Now all such questions like how do you remove yourself from this system, how to track your money, how to know where you are wasting money, and how you get rid of 3rd party debt will now be clearly addressed in front of you. You will never have to finance another purchase with other people's money. Let's understand this in-depth.

It's more about how you utilize your income or present wealth in generating future wealth. No matter if you are earning $500 or $5000 a week, all it matters is how you are spending, saving, and investing that money. Having a solid strategic plan can save you from a lot of unwanted spending. It can guide you to suitable investments and make your financial goals more stable. It will not only cover you from bad finance but also help you become an independent strategist.

## You need a System that isn't BROKEN!

A wall street corrupt system is not what you or your family deserve. A system where you can be your own master, driver, and controller is what you really need. A broken system controls you and your decisions, while the other gives you the liberty to take your actions, become independent and become financially literate.

Sometimes having a broken system is far more dangerous than having no system at all.

It's the same here! Think like that, you want to run a shoe factory, but you don't have the right labor with a related skill set, you have obsolete machines, you have resources that aren't suitable to run the factory. And after all of this, you are finally starting with the shoe production. Do you think you will be able to get the best results? Will you be able to take orders or deliver them on time? If the system is at fault, how will you manage to generate revenue? Give away salaries or even cover the costs?

Yes, indeed, a broken system can't do it at all. You need to fix things asap. You need to learn, organize and manage things properly. You have to streamline operations and put them to their best use. Remember that you are only creating more obstacles for your growth with a broken system.

It goes the same in the financial system. If there are so many loopholes in the financial journey, how will you make the best out of it? It will be a total loss. It's like trying to swim in the choppy waters; knowingly, it isn't possible. Why am I telling you to understand the system? It is because I want you to know everything about it so that no one can trick you. No one can make you a fool again.

Imagine that you have to go somewhere, but you don't know the address, will you be able to make it there on time? You may ask someone for directions, those directions can be right or wrong, but a lot of help is required to reach that exact direction. It can be too messy and problematic for you. So, your chances of getting lost are extremely high.

## Connecting the Dots of your Financial Mapping

How can you prevent yourself from getting lost? It's simple. Get a map, follow that map, connect the dots and reach your destination. A map can be an ultimate guide for you. Have you ever seen people who hike or travel often? They always have a map with them. The same goes for financial planning. You have to have a map for you.

## Understanding the Financial Journey and its Mapping

See, everyone's financial journey is different. Not everyone is heading in the same direction. While you have another financial goal, your friend will have a different one. Everyone's priorities are different. So, it depends on what kind of financial plans you have. Some people want to build a home; some are looking for a lazy retirement plan, some are planning a wedding for their children, and some want to make enough wealth for their grandchildren.

Everyone has a dream to fulfill, and I know that when all your life, you work hard and you want to spend the rest of it stress-free, money is very important at that time. But the end goal for everyone remains the same. It is to make wealth, good wealth, and escape all the debts. No one wants to die, thinking they have debts to cover. You see why a customized financial plan is required here. We do this for our clients for free. Insane right?

If you are willing to reach your financial destination, you must know about the obstacles, time, and how much wealth you have right now. If you don't know your challenges, how can you succeed in making wealth? That's the point of understanding the financial system with a map.

Just like in a map, you will know when the next milestone arrives; it goes the same with your financial journey with an Infinite Wealth Strategist.

The dots are those milestones that we want to achieve for you. Those dots are connecting dots; you have to join them on time and make the best of them.

## Who will usher you to the destination?

Do you know what is the biggest challenge people face is when it comes to their financial future? They may not know how much they should be saving or what kind of investments are best for them, making things difficult down the road.

I know that you are intelligent and capable of making your own decisions, but somewhere down the line, we all need someone to guide and enlighten us about what's right and wrong. Managing finances can be a daunting task that can keep you involved in detail, which I don't like personally. Though our Vortex Banking System doesn't consist of the rigged system,it is flexible and agile. It works according to your situation.

The Financial Mapping Strategist of Infinite Wealth Strategist is a specialized individual who will be your right hand! They are all licensed agents of the highest caliber and integrity. They will help you identify and prioritize your financial goals, create a plan to make those goals happen, and provide the tools, information, and support to get there. It's important to make the right financial decisions that will set you up for success today and in the future.

It's equally important to maximize all earning potential while minimizing any risks associated with investing your hard-earned money. It is the reason why our team of seasoned professionals has what it takes to make these difficult choices between maximizing gains or reducing risk.

Our team will take on all your questions, no need for you to worry about a thing! One primary concern many people today have regarding their finances-from where I invest my money, what am I investing in? What's worth buying at any given time?

These are just some examples, but there are plenty more out there. Fortunately, our team has got you covered with experts who could answer these concerns and help pave your way through life financially.

LiveIWS Financial Mapping Tool will get you to your end goal! All you have to do is follow it!

liveiws.com

Sometimes I wonder, if I had this choice in my initial days of financial education, things would have been different.

Today, bank professionals will not even look at you if you go to banks and you don't have a ton of money with them. They think that a common man is undeserving of any notice or explanation. How foolish of us to believe that those bank officials are more intelligent than us. Remember we talked about financial literacy?

No, not financial education, but financial literacy makes the difference and draws the line. If you are financially aware of the very basics in life, no one can take away your economic right from you. I remember this one time staring for long at a piece of the bank's document and thought, why do we have to agree with a system that doesn't agree with us. It doesn't support us at all.

The financial mapping strategists are well-versed people. They can take you to deeper insights and show you the reality. They won't tell you things for the sake of it but rather support you in all the best possible ways. They master the financial art and can create the most suitable cash flow optimization strategy for you. That one incredible thing about them is listening to all your financial queries and providing a holistic financial system based on those solutions. I mean, if you get someone to guide you to better and without any selfish means, isn't it the best thing?

A few days back, I was in a conversation with someone, and it went really well. We discussed the financial growth of an individual and how in life, at some point, we should be having this much wealth and this much after we have passed a certain age.

Our conversation covered different perspectives, and it was enthralling to see how that youngster was feeling at that time. I could see his willingness to learn about financial strategies to scale wealth. The whole conversation was very interactive, and I concluded three points from it.

The first one was that youngster was full of hopes and dreams, but directionless. Second, he wanted someone to guide him and to show him the way. Third, he has a standard mind makeup of the financial banking system. These three things for a youngster can leave him in an absolute mess. He can be left hopeless, which is why many youngsters don't take financial independence positively. It's more like a risk.

It is a risk that can change their lives, but they are too unsure about it. I am against these financial restrictions that youngsters feel. When you are young, you should have all the economic liberty to access the monetary decision-making of your life. Such mindsets can put you down, just like the young fellow who has so many dreams but feels so helpless. This is sad and we need to start educating our children because the system has them in their sweaty grips! This has to change!

## Why do you need an IWS Mapping Strategy?

Let's assume that the average American household has $15,000 in credit card debt and $40,000 in student loan debt.

Most Americans live paycheck-to-paycheck and have no extra money to invest in their future or the future of their children. They will never retire early because they don't have a plan.

IWS MAPPING STRATEGY is a proven way to get out of debt quickly, put more money into your pocket every month and create cash flow so you can finally invest for retirement and set up an inheritance fund for your kids. We show you how to do it with our Debt Snowball Calculator that shows you EXACTLY what day you'll be out of debt AND how much time and money saved along the way!

Imagine that when we have our families, and we all have responsibilities to fulfill, how can we even take a financial risk at that time?

It's essential to make the right financial decisions that will set you up for success today and in the future. Our Financial Mapping Strategists specialize in Cash Flow Optimization. This strategy will maximize all earning potential while minimizing any risks associated with investing your hard-earned money, which is why our team of seasoned

liveiws.com

professionals has what it takes to make these difficult choices between maximizing gains or reducing risk.

Our Financial Mapping Strategist can help you handle your financial situation. They will create an action plan that's uniquely tailored to your goals, personal needs, and finances, so every penny is being put to good use! They'll walk you step-by-step through a roadmap they've created. When you invest in your future, it is important to make sure you are not wasting money. A Financial Road Map will help establish financial progress and reduce expenses so that there's more room for growth investments.

A Financial Roadmap can be used as a guide on how to reach your goals by identifying potential pitfalls before they happen or stumbling blocks where things could go wrong with the right guidance from an expert who knows what needs attention first and last because of their experience working through similar situations many times over.

Let me tell you how our Banking Practices are different from Traditional Banking Practices:

The Typical Equity Mutual Fund Investor has only earned 3.98% annually for the past 31 years! He has beaten inflation by just 1.3% a year while there were all kinds of risks involved in this long financial journey!

According to DALBAR 2012, Asset Allocation and Fixed Income, Investors actually lost when factoring in the cost of inflation.

A recent survey by the Federal Reserve indicated that a sudden expense could force them to do things that may not turn out right for them. Just over $400 would move most American families to practically begging, borrow or sell anything they have to cover up their expenses. We have also discussed this above. This monetary system is debt-based and rigged. It is designed to keep the average American family vulnerable. Can you think of the actual condition that Americans are surviving in? It exposes the ongoing financial "set-backs."

Do you know? Four out of Five Mutual Funds and Investment advisory services underperform every year? The reason is that the overall market over the long-term course does not provide them with suitable growth factors. Of course, there are so many players, and if money pours in, everyone will be financially sufficient. But this is against the standard banking laws.

According to an AARP survey report, Anxiety Index SurveyWell, Wall Street lost more than 50% of the typical investors' money! Not once but twice! The year was 1999. As a result, 73% of all baby Boomers now believe that they will have to postpone retirement because they can afford just to get by. It is so disheartening to see how people are fooled and manipulated all their lives.

I am sharing some factual information with you here because, as a person, you can doubt things, and it is normal. Our system is an evolving system because it has been noticed almost after years. So, facts can help you understand why Vortex Banking is not only important but crucial for your growth. Well, our strategies are a proven alternative that can help you take back control of your financial future! Our strategies provide the three things traditional investments cannot offer: Guaranteed Growth, Capital Preservation, and Security. We can help you take back control of your financial future!

Investing in stocks, bonds, and mutual funds can be a great way to grow your wealth. However, they cannot compare with the peace of mind or guaranteed growth that Infinite Banking Strategies provide by default! That's because our strategies are contractually guaranteed to grow annually by a predictable amount year after year without interruptions or hidden tax implications.

## Why so much Buzz about Infinite Wealth Strategist? LiveIWS.com

No one can predict the future, but with an IWS Banking System in place, you'll be able to create a stable financial foundation for your family and friends. With the IWS System, you can create growing financial capital to fund your necessities without worrying about where it will come from. Your money grows in a secure environment while earning interest and potentially dividends! Our banking strategies are designed for individuals who recognize that even in today's digital age, there can still be unforeseen challenges and opportunities.

There may come a time when your current strategy just doesn't cut it anymore or isn't able to keep up with how fast life changes around us. So don't wait until something bad happens- have an ongoing plan of attack, so nothing catches you off guard!

Owning a bank account has many benefits, including earning interest on your money and having access to it at any time. It is because we guarantee that customers can withdraw their funds tax-free from banks without being charged for withdrawing them in cash or transferring them into another form of payment such as checks.

Plus, if you have an emergency fund just sitting there not doing anything but collecting dust every month while carrying all kinds of fees and penalties, why not put it somewhere where you will earn more than what those outdated savings accounts offer?

In addition to these perks are the security measures banks take with customer information, so they never need to fear someone accessing sensitive data like credit card numbers through hacking attacks since banking institutions encrypt everything, which leaves no room for third party intervention.

We've all heard people say that they're a little bit too scared to invest in the stock market. But what about when our own banks are crashing? When you can't trust your own bank? It becomes too risky to give up your life savings to something that doesn't even promise a safe return. America has lost trillions of dollars, and banking can't pay it back because their assets have plummeted as well!

We ensure that you don't lose your money, hard earned wealth and assets - so we don't only let you save up for emergencies with an emergency fund but multiply wealth with given resources? With Infinite

Wealth strategies, all you have to do is outline your financial goals and make targets.

The buzz about this particular strategy is not because it belonged to the riches, and now it is ours. It is because it has credibility, can be trusted, and can guide you towards financial progress. People who have tried it are happy and satisfied. One fantastic thing that surprises me about the strategy is that it gives way to learn and create a legacy of your own. The riches had a culture of finance. They knew how to use even 1% of their wealth to operate correctly.

Imagine if you could put 50% of your wealth in the right place, how much money you can get in return. The strategy has some solid logic that can benefit the masses. Vortex Bankingis brilliant in its approach. If you go deep and learn about their working mechanism, you will understand its significance in a person's life. This book again is to get you to see the concept and our strategists job is to set you up and teach you how to implement it into your life!

## Now, are you ready to fire your traditional banker and BE THE BANKER yourself?

I expect the answer to be yes! With all evidence and facts, it is time to understand that your finances will be under your control when you become the bank. Your wealth will multiply and grow in time. Let's read further to get more clarity on this part. I hope you have understood the mapping strategy, our strategies, and the possibility of financing your purchase till now.

When Robert Kiyosaki said that We are programmed to be Poor, it was a believable reality. It was so powerful that I could relate to this whole line very well. It is like someone has deep-rooted words like 'You can't be Rich' in our minds, and we can't seem to overcome it. How disgusting does it sound? How many people in life always tell you that you can't be wealthy? In my early journey it seemed everyone around me wanted me to fail. I don't know about you but when someone tells me I'll fail, I ensure that I won't!

It's indeed hard to make ends meet, especially in this economy. I don't know a single person who doesn't have their own financial struggles and feels like they never save enough for retirement because of how much it costs just to live day-to-day life. Who do you know that lives paycheck to paycheck, month to month? The only way they can pay their bills is by using credit cards. They're just one emergency away from being in major debt and becoming another statistic! How many times have you felt like your financial situation controls your life?

Financial struggles are a constant reality for many people. It's difficult to save money, make financial decisions and feel like you have control over your life when the never-ending cycle of living paycheck to paycheck fails them every time. But when you become your bank with LiveIWS, everything turns upside down! Tables turn, and you can't believe what happens when you follow the system!

It feels almost like magic to have your bank account grow with each deposit. Of course, it does not happen overnight, and you will need to invest wisely for the money to impact your life in a substantial way, but as long as you remain patient, there is no limit on what wealth can do for your family.

Wealth often comes from unexpected places or people, especially when passed down through generations. One way that VortexBanking facilitates this process: because of their longevity, these institutions help families keep generational assets together so those cultural traditions may be able (and continue) throughout many different eras.

## But let's first understand the problems with traditional banking and Infinite Wealth Strategist's benefits.

The traditional banking and retirement plans are not as great as they seem. They're problematic for several reasons, including no principal protection; guaranteed growth is non-existent; credit checks to borrow money from the bank or other institutions means you can't get easy access to your funds without some kind of verification in place first - management fees that many banks charge on top make them even less attractive - finally, there's also potential tax liability if heirs inherit these accounts when we die because all our hard work could be taxed again!

Many people are unhappy with traditional banking and retirement plans that have a slew of drawbacks, including no principal protection, no guaranteed growth, credit checks to borrow money, management fees, and the lack of any protection from creditors or potential for the tax liability. Withdrawals come out taxed too!

I will tell you how traditional banking ruthlessness has come to my attention. I used to think my retirement plan would just be a little bit of money I could pull out whenever I wanted. Still, nowadays, with all the security breaches and other recent major events in our country's financial system, it seems like you can't even trust your bank.

The first thing that bothered me is when they said there was no principal protection on traditional savings accounts or C.D.s. You're at risk for losing every penny if something bad happens because they don't offer any guarantees against losses from market downturns, inflation rates increasing faster than interest rates, etcetera!

Next up was how risky those investments are- what guarantee does anyone have? Then came credit checks to borrow money; management fees charged by banks; not having protection from creditors.

While on the other side, imagine what your life would be like if you were rich enough to stop working. Imagine how much time and energy it would free up for really important things - spending more time with family, traveling the world, doing whatever you want! You can spend quality time doing your favorite things. You can escape the rat race and enjoy it to the fullest. Do ministry full time with no worries about money. Life wasn't given to us to slave for others while we end up with scraps!

# Take the Final Call!

The Infinite Wealth Strategies Are designed specifically for people who have always dreamed of becoming self-made millionaires but never knew where to start or just didn't think they had the right skillset. This isn't some get-rich-quick scheme; this is an investment in yourself and your future success, as well as financial security, should anything happen today, so don't wait another second before putting these strategies into action! You deserve infinite wealth too!

Infinite Wealth Strategist has a revolutionary financial system option that can give you all the "best-banking" features without any risk. With 100% principal protection, guaranteed growth, and no credit checks to borrow money, it makes Infinite

Wealth Strategist the most secure way for investors who want peace of mind with their investments!

There's no risk involved with any part of this plan. Plus, YOU will be in control every step along the way as well: just sit back & watch how much money starts coming into YOUR life without having to do anything at all by yourself!

The 401(k) is one of the most popular ways to save for retirement. However, it's not without its drawbacks and disadvantages that actuarial science can help you avoid!

The process by which we retire from working life has changed significantly in recent decades - but regrettably, this isn't always a good thing. For starters, there's no guarantee your money will grow at all if left with Wall Street Greed and speculation; furthermore, when retired people withdraw their funds, they may be subjected to taxes as well as penalties too! By investing wisely instead of using math studies combined with statistics, however, you'll know exactly how much income-tax-free passive income you should expect every year while saving more than ever before on top of guaranteeing 100% growth.

I want all of us to retire with peace of mind, knowing your money is safe.

Here's a little-known secret. You have equity in your home that you could be using to help build yourself an unbeatable retirement nest egg, and it doesn't require any new borrowing or risky investments. LiveIWS teaches people of all ages how they can use their unspent surplus from years past to turbocharge what's already sitting right under their noses: the value of their homes! And because this strategy involves no riskier equities investing, there are zero downsides.

liveiws.com

Life is full of surprises, but your retirement should not be one of them. With Tax-Free Retirement, you can know exactly if and when you can retire with guaranteed lifetime income - without fear that any creditors will take it away from you! It's simple: all the interest on your money is 100% tax deductible which means no more paying taxes for anything else in life or worrying about whether there'll still be enough left over at the end. Plus, our plan allows for creditor protection, so they never get their hands on what matters most (your hard-earned salary). If this sounds like a perfect solution, then go ahead and contact us today before anyone catches wind because we're limited due time offer expires soon, just as everyone takes advantage.

## It is time for you to start asking some serious questions!

Do you want to take your financial life into YOUR OWN hands? To make the decisions about where, when, and how much money goes out of or comes in for your family's needs? Do you know someone who wants that level of control over their finances but doesn't have it because they are too busy with work or don't understand how to do those tasks independently?

The thing is, there's a lot more than just budgets going on behind the scenes every day - interest rates changing (sometimes without warning), inflation eating away at our savings. It can be overwhelming! And if we're not careful, these things might happen while we're driving home from work one day-then suddenly everything changes. It could mean losing hundreds of valuable money!

Imagine having the ability to recapture all of your expenses while paying off your debt completely and building a tax-free lifetime income!

# What benefits will you receive from Infinite Wealth Strategists?

Your Authorized Wealth Strategist will help you identify your key goals and answer any questions on a one-on-one basis.

Your Authorized Wealth Strategist will create a Personalized Solution that shows you how The Vortex BankingSystem can help you reach your primary goals. Keep in mind, though, that each policy is custom designed. There is no one-size-fits-all policy!

It can be tough to manage your money, but our Wealth Strategists are masters at helping you restructure your finances so that it's not an issue.

Based on initial and ongoing planning with our Wealth Strategist, we'll help make sure that putting some extra cash from these policies towards any other goal is something that will work out well in the long-term - whether it's a new car, tuition costs at an expensive school or additional funds when they are needed most.

We have focused on developing such a system to strengthen every common person's dream, which looked long and hard until we discovered the Vortex Banking System.

All the greedy bankers who are eyeing your investment prospects and money will not trouble you anymore. You don't have to work on their will but you can now make your own decisions. Remember that no one knows the best use of their financial assets and money except you. Reducing debt and increasing cash flow is so much better than you might have thought. Today with Infinite Wealth Strategist, it will become actual and possible. The tools we use to enhance wealth are incredible, tested, and have produced excellent outcomes for several people like you and me.

I know you've been saving for emergencies. You probably have a lot of money sitting in your bank account that's just waiting to be used, but there are so many other things tempting it away right now! Spend some time thinking about what could happen if an emergency arises and how much is needed before deciding on the amount you can afford to put aside each month. You will be assisted by our strategists and develop more potential financial strategies for your benefit.

Imagine a future where you leave behind more than just memories. With the right investment, secure your legacy for generations to come and live out this goal. Enjoy an independent financial life and control finances the way you want to and not by someone's pathetic guidance.

It's shocking how much we're paying for money that doesn't even belong to us. It seems like the whole world is just obsessed with borrowing and lending, but at what point does it become too expensive? We could be looking in all sorts of places when deciding where to save our hard-earned cash - maybe a neighbor or family member needs help (or wants out), their company might need some investment, they may have found an opportunity overseas.

The one-percenters have used their wealth to create a legacy for generations. At Infinite Wealth Strategist, we can teach you the strategies they use and have used to not get stuck here on earth while your descendants live large in space!

The more you work, the less time your money spends sitting in a bank account. By owning a banking system and properly protecting your assets, you create an investment structure that allows for compounding interest to work as hard as it can so they'll be able to make even better investments on behalf of future generations.

I understand that your mind is now trying to streamline a lot of information at once, but the information you have read so far is very important for you.

Honestly, all the wealthiest families use the Vortex Banking System and tools to create massive amounts of wealth. The trickiest part is they have been doing this for a long time now, but they had no clue that someday, we will also get to know about it. The Elite NEVER earned money because they did a lot of hard work. They earned money because they saved right, invested properly, and utilized their money sensibly. They knew about the government's tactics, and that's the reason they kept on multiplying their wealth. Next time, if someone tells you, you can't be rich! Laugh in their face and remember there is always a way to succeed!

Suppose you are willing to change your financial future and want to become financially independent. Infinite Wealth Strategist is where you need to look for assistance. It's your wealth, and no one can take that from you. This book is dedicated to giving you a complete understanding of what, why, and how Infinite Wealth Strategist is changing the traditional ways of earning and converting them into more advanced strategies that are up with the times!

Let's make the best use of this opportunity and start today. It's not that I want you to become rich in a day, but I want you to grow enough wealth that it doesn't leave you disappointed. When you don't manage your money properly, it can be hard to break away from debt chains. That's why we're here for you--to help!

The best way to start taking control is by learning how and when to take that first step to manage your finances. With Infinite Wealth Strategist, it's time that you finally make the decision and connect with our specialists. It's going to be a revolutionary upgrade, something you have always dreamt of.

We are known as the Global Leader in Asset Protection and are here to give you peace of mind. With our patented, copyrighted financial instrument, your assets are protected from lawsuits, judgments, and bypass estate taxes with ease. Honestly, the government gives you some pretty awesome incentives if you're in the real estate business, investment, and working somewhere else. You'll be able to avoid capital gains when purchasing or selling property and defer income tax! Speak with your Wealth Strategist; he can help assess whether these benefits are available for YOU!

Finally, I am putting my thoughts to rest and heading towards a leap of faith. I am glad that I could share all this information with you, and now, you are going to share the same with other people around you, I hope.

I know that whatever you have right now is enough to generate more wealth. I know you will look deeper into generating more wealth now that you have been enlightened. And, look, I am confident about it! But, all I want to tell you is that your one decision can change several lives. Ask your doubts, queries, and questions. I am here to give you complete guidance and end-to-end assistance on anything you want to know. This is my passion as well as the person who shared this book with you. We are on your team and we are here to ensure your success!

I will always help you, so feel comfortable coming to me or any of our strategists. At LiveIWS our clients become our family. It's one life, and you are going to make it BIG! That's my promise!

liveiws.com